Out of Tune

John Hartley

Published by Broken Down Books, 2023.

OUT OF TUNE

First edition. May 6, 2023.

ISBN: 979-8223412816

Written by John Hartley.

Table of Contents

With much gratitude to Garry, Tony, Andrew, Matt, John, Jon, John, Jason, and Vicky

Introduction

These words have been selected quite carefully. They have been selected carefully now, just as they have been selected carefully at various points over the past three decades or so. At the time, they were selected for the way they fitted tunes in my head; tunes which would become, with the addition of these words, songs. These songs were then recorded in a variety of locations with a variety of people on a variety of occasions. The one constant is that they were written by Johny Nocash.

Johny Nocash was born in the late 1980s, into the body of a teenager growing up in the industrial north west of England. His hometown, once agricultural, later founded on weaving and coal, was now more akin to overspill for the continued expansion of Manchester. His parents were working class, one trained as a teacher before finding a spiritual home and workplace in the library; the other trained as a tailor's cutter, rose through middle management, then chose to carry coffins and put his tailoring skills to practical use in the embalming trade. Johny was proud - is proud of the background in which he grew up. Money was never abundant, but neither did the family go hungry. Sacrifices were made - a car-less family for several years, the local phone box was as good a way of communicating as writing a letter and seemed to suffice, Live Aid was watched in black and white - but the importance of education and family was never compromised.

The teenage boy into whose body Johny Nocash was born did not have a name that was going to set the world alight, that was going to capture people's imaginations. History shows that the pseudonym didn't do that either, but it was a fair enough attempt. Inspired by a combination of a love of music, a love of puns, a nod to a member of the band Chumbawamba, and of financial reality, Johny Nocash first came to the public's attention via Westhoughton's finest (only?) political-pop-busking duo the Fabricators. With Garry, he made his first visit to a recording studio and for the first time heard one of his songs recorded properly, rather than on a cassette recorder in front of the bar fire in Garry's front room on a Sunday morning.

Johny branched out, and in the dregs of his university days headed back to the same studio, nestling in the junction of Pennines and Peaks, to record songs under the name the Irony Board. This story has been documented in full in *Capturing the Wry*, but in a nutshell: Johny wrote songs, had record label interest, formed a proper band with his cousin and his friend, made a video, added another friend to the band, recorded more, fell in love and moved south. There endeth the Irony Board.

Ensconced in the south, a self-styled infiltrator from within, Johny continued to write songs. He found gainful employment in the field of special education, befriended several other people called John and accidentally formed a band called Echolalia. This story has been documented in full in *Welcome to the Underachievers*, but in a nutshell: Johny was friends with Jacques, they recorded some songs on a portastudio , enjoyed it, decided to play a gig, busked, performed to around 200 people, had record label interest, recorded in 16-tracks, Jacques disappeared, Johny became disillusioned, the band played a rainwashed-out festival, Johny gave up and didn't tell anybody. There endeth Echolalia.

Life continued apace. His own family grew, he watched his home suck in a car through its brick walls, he felt extended family bereavement, he put his head down and worked hard, leaving the slippery slopes of Further Education for the more secure compulsory school sector, teaching and leading in special education. He continued to write songs. He deliberately formed a band that wasn't a band, taking its name from Mrs

Nocash's suggestion having read an article by John Peel in the *Radio Times*: Broken Down Lorry. He recorded songs on his own portastudio, reconnected with Jacques and recorded an album on eight-track, bought his own eight-track, recorded more, had music released by short-run record labels, had an album ready for further release and then ... the label went quiet. Silent, even. There endeth Broken Down Lorry.

Life continued apace. Johny amused himself by creating further alter egos. Inspired by KLF-er and artist Bill Drummond's tale of releasing a 7" single by a fictional Norwegian band (even going to Norway to record it), Johny set his sights closer to home: the island of Alderney. Johny wrote a fictional seven-song taster CD featuring songs from seven fictional artists recording for a fictional record label based on the tiny island (population circa 1800). He distributed the CD incognito to his extended family, who enjoyed the joke. He wrote *Searching for the Sound of Riduna*, a novel based on the sampler CD. He wrote and recorded more songs by the various artists, drawing in rare contributions from his family for added authenticity and variety. He serialised a fictional diary for a website, *Dukla Prague Away Kit*, for which he also wrote music reviews and content.

By now, Johny wasn't feeling very well, the trials and tribulations of life and experience that had been soaked up now leaving the sponge at saturation point. He began to play piano (left hand, one finger, right hand three fingers and occasionally a tentative fourth) to help get his brain back on track. He wrote some songs and released them on a CD under the name the Broken Heed. The CD raised money for a charity, and with his social media friend John he put on a fundraising gig in Huddersfield, raising even more money. He recorded and released a second album, although he had hoped he wouldn't need to. He began to feel better. Johny continued to write songs and write about songs. He started writing for the website *Everything Indie Over 40*, and then for the website *Toppermost*. He continued to record songs, on his own eight-track studio, and during the global pandemic and national lockdown of 2020 released some of these under his own name.

The words selected within this book are Johny's words, written at various times during a period lasting over thirty years. They are presented here as writing in its own right, stripped of instrumental accompaniment, for your reading pleasure. The words are selected, out of tune.

John Hartley, February 2023.

Bus Stop Bravado

This is my life story
It's mundane and dead boring
I can't seem to stop yawning and I feel a bit ashamed
With beer belly blues and scuffled shoes
I walk through suburban avenues
I think too much and get confused and I waste my time away
I'm torn apart and bored to tears
Waiting for something to appear
But I've been waiting over twenty years
It'd try the patience of the best man
Never mind an also-ran
I knew as I walked the old estate
That I'd made a big mistake
But not even a guilty conscience could help keep me awake

TLLS

There's a tender little love song
has our name on its lips
but I can't say you'd notice
cos we don't ever kiss
as we fall into love
we fall out of bed
when we fall for each other
are we easily led?
There's a tender little love song
that I sing in my head
And I can't say I've listened
to a word that you've said
as we fall out of love
it falls into place
and I can't stop you smiling
cos I don't know which face
There's a tender little love song
has our names in tattoo
something to remind us
we had nothing better to do
as we fall out of love
I fall to the floor
and fall with you throwing rocks at my door

Monty (What Have You Done?)

Monty
What have you done?
You've left the children in the sun
And forgot about the frost
And now a line's been crossed.
Monty, I would forgive you
If I ever had the heart
One day I will forgive you ...
The reminders we planted here
Have surfaced over there
Amnesiacal ferals
Must have mined this metre square
One day I'll claim this land as my own
Monty
What have you done?
You've left the children in the sun
And forgot about the frost
And now a line's been crossed
Monty
I would forgive you
If I ever had the heart
One day I will forgive you
That's a start.

It Looks Like We're Done For

You take the left hand
And I'll take the right hand
Given time, we'll dance our way across the floor
It looks like we're done for
I'm getting tired of being battered
Getting tired of being hammered
Next time I might not be back for more
You say I'm static
A man automatic
Harsh words have sometimes led into a war
It looks like we're done for
I'd say I'm lacking
In thought and in planning
Truth is, I'm being eaten to the core
It looks like we're done for

A Friend in Elvis

When you're diving for pearls at the bottom of the world
Remember: you can't get any lower
When you're on the escalator up to Heaven's gate
Remember: it's a natural high
When you're staring at the walls like you've never stared before
Remember: you've always been good looking
And with beauty on your side but still no sign of bride
Maybe it's time to give it up
When you haven't got a halo and everything you touch turns to stone
You've got a friend in Elvis
Just pick up the phone
You can call me up
I will take you home
We can talk for hours and hours and hours
If you call me up
I will take you home
We can talk for hours and hours and hours
You can call me
Call me

The Most Powerful Man in the World

The past does my head in
I can hear your engine revving
And I swear we were together
In my dream
It seems I've got the strangest power
I could keep you here for hours
Waiting for my sign to turn to green
I'm happy that I've found you
In truth I never tried to
But now I have I'd like to keep in touch
I haven't got a fortune
But I'd burn my telly for you
As romance goes I know that isn't much
You could take me home
Untie the strings
Give me food
Keep me warm
But I'll never be a superstar
I'm no Mark Lamarr
I never get the girl

Shoegazing

In time
You will understand me
In time
This time
You lay the boots in
Hard
This time
It doesn't matter
The book
You're reading has
No words
The song
You're singing has
No verse
Intrigue
Is something that you've learned
Mystique
Is what I didn't

The Death of a Pigeon

Billy got impaled on the spikes,
Jilly shot down mid-flight
Phil, he ate his feet to survive
This is no life
Kenny got electric-shocked,
Jenny separated from the flock
And Pele,
well he flew in front of a bus
This is no life
This is no life
"Settle down with a nest and a wife,
It'll be all right!"
But nothing works how you want it to
I can't do what I want to do
And a quick one upon the lamppost
Is all I can look forward to
I dodge your toddler throwing stones
I chew Kentucky Fried Chicken bones
Born and ate and died alone
So make it quick and easy
Find a cage to release me
Find a kestrel to decease me

Ten Minutes in a Hot Bath

There's a kiss in your eye
What I see I don't like
I've been here before and
You left me
High and dry
I counted out the hours and days
Until you'd gone
But I can't sit in silence
When I don't know what is wrong
I dodged the boots
And wedding suits to bring you home
And now I'm thick because I don't understand
Vent your spleen until it bursts
Spit out all those hateful words
I can't soak them like a sponge
You bleed me dry
And when all is said and done
You'll be the first to hit and run
I'll bide my time and rue the day
So we get what we deserve
Willie Nelson's got a nerve
There's no glory in the tin
It's just scum and surf

Where the Sun Doesn't Shine

I've got a feeling I need to unwind
Sit back, relax and watch the tide
In the summer I wear my feet down
In the winter I put them up
I've got a feeling I need to unwind
Sit back, relax and watch the tide
In the summer sometimes I get high
In the winter I just get by
I'm going where the sun doesn't shine

Any Good Ideas?

Take me away
Lead me astray
I can't stay another day
If you look
Closely
In the corner
That's me:
The deadwood of the family tree
In a rut above the rest
With an empty treasure chest
I tried my hardest
Take it as read
It's a fraying thread
That I'm pinning my hopes on
I'll do what I do best
I'll give a pound of flesh
And a penny to the wiseguy
I feel second rate
Everybody's two-faced
And the answer
Lies behind my back
I feel ill at ease
I need remedies
Have you any good ideas?

Lost

It's windy outside
It's warm in here
With the TV on
And my can of beer
My wings are stained and
Smell of piss
My halo rusted in the mist
But I've devised a way to cope
I call my strategy 'no hope'
When things go wrong
As they sometimes do
I play my harp and dream of you
When I was buried out at sea
You thought you'd seen the back of me
But I came back
Cos I got lost
You should have
Nailed me to a cross

The Circus

I'll run away
I'll run away
I'll be gone by the morning
Won't leave you any warning
I'll run away
I'll run away
I'll sneak out by the back door
There's a note left by the front door
I ran away
I'm coming back
I'm coming back
The trouble with the circus is you only scratch the surface
It's not just tents and campfires
There's a lot more to the high wire

Lie

Maybe you shouldn't wake me in the morning
There's so many secrets I can't keep
Maybe you should walk away without a warning
Maybe it's a climb I find too steep ...
I've not felt too good about things lately
There's so much to do that I don't do
You're asking for a change that isn't likely
Or maybe it's a change that's just begun
While there's a chance that I've tuned the corner
There's a chance I'm going round the bend
And there's a chance that everyone's a gonner
And there's a chance that this is not the end
Would you lie to me?

The Last Will and Testament

Left on the floor in one thousand pieces
Walked over, trodden on folds and creases
Frayed at the edges with a hole in the middle
Candle-wax stains over words that mattered
Fragile little thoughts that are ripped and tattered
This is the way I left it all to you
Two hundred quid stuffed inside the sofa
Gas stove, kettle and electric toaster
Boxes of photos (don't know who they are…)
300 discs of collectable vinyl
12 inch, 7 inch - no Richie, Lionel –
I may be old but I've still got pride
Found on the floor in a thousand pieces
Matched up, taped up, ironed-out creases
Tear-stained words with a heart in the middle
Candle wax stains over names that married
Tender little gifts for the children carried,
Loved and left, but not forgotten

Detrimental Detectors

No time to get sentimental
It's detrimental to my health
I can't say I ever got my way
Now or ever
Never being one to like the difficult
I'm still waiting for you to pick me up
I feel crestfallen
You gave no warning
Now or ever
Got the sack - please, take me back -
All my belongings in a carrier bag
No time to get bleary-eyed
Now or ever
Won't take me back
Just pulling me backwards
The clock ticks and tocks
So melodramatic
Excited about the eyesore
I have seen the detrimental detectors

Merry Christmas. Don't Make a Fuss. Part One.

The sky above is laden with snow
All dressed up and nowhere to go
One more Christmas, one more no-show
The sound of church bells whispers in the air
You tease the tinsel out of your hair
Whilst your mascara's running everywhere
There's nothing I can say to stop the hurt
Just wipe away your tears with my shirt
As I wrap my arms around you
Merry Christmas
Don't make a fuss

Merry Christmas. Don't Make a Fuss. Part Two.

We fall hook, line and sinker
As we fail to see the plot:
We all spend too much money,
(more money than we'd got)
Then we'll all sing the same songs
Though we're not sure of the words
That one about that fairytale ...
We'll look towards the future
We'll toast to absent friends
And try to make the Advent candle
Burn out at both ends
And when Mary came from two doors down
We'll say a little prayer
For grandad in his eiderdown
Tradition says be merry
With a serpent in your tree
Are all those fruits and berries as much for Yule as me?
Let's give a nod to Saturn
As we hang up your wreath
If you scratch away at Christmas
What lies beneath?

Breathe

I can't sleep
I can't breath
In this house
The breeze creaks in
It sucks the air from my mouth
The outlook is bleak
The winds of change
Have changed
They blew me out
I'm not getting any younger
I can't sleep
I can't breathe
In this house
The trees creep in
Their roots invade my mouth

Capturing the Wry

Foresight
Is a wonderful asset
But I see what I see now
Through rose-tinted glasses
I only reminisce
About the things I miss
Because it's easy.
I've seen you smiling
At leisure
You say that I can too
I say never
I find it much more fun
To seem to be having
None
But that's just me
The coastline harbours our secrets
The seawall's not the be-all or the end
If I seem to close up
In the open season
And you can't get in
It's because
I can't get to grips
With the slippery slopes
While you reign supreme
I'll end up soaked
You can go your way
And I'll go mine
I'll thumb a lift
While you
Toe the line

And this is a sight
For my sore eyes
This is the worst to which I am wise
You can play Twister
I will shout
"Ann!
Have no doubts!
I'm on my way out."

Rockets in the Sky

Reeling
From a high of uselessness
Go I
One look from you
I'm lost for words
But I'll get by
Just don't ask why
I took a bad start
And made it worse
It's all peaks
And troughs
A hiccup
A cough
And awkward silence can
Resume
But I'll get by
There but for the grace of God
Go I
Doctor Deadbeat, you'll presume
I can't decide
If they're rockets
In the sky?
Am I dead?
Am I alive?
Have none of us survived?
And if living on the moon
Won't explain my lunacy
Maybe I'd be sane
If I lived in your galaxy

Just Give the Man an Allotment

Steel grey sky
It's the middle of July
Don't ask
Why I can't look you in the eye
Chase the voices from my head
Chase them living
Chase them dead
Give me shovel
Give me spade
Keep me warm on winter day
Give me vegetables
And shed
I want salt of earth instead
Pebbledash rain
Flicker of old flame
Will an allotment keep me sane?
Or will I lose the plot again?

Ifs

If
I wasn't
Gagged and bound
If
You earned
A few more pounds
If
We didn't
Decorate our paths with eggshells
And if
Life was
Made of cotton
Would our love
Be strong or rotten?
And if
Life was
Love abundant
Would we find ourselves
Redundant?

Fingers

Give me fingers
Give me bone
Give me possessions
Give me home
I always wanted to be someone
You couldn't see
I never wanted to be
Someone

A Furnished Field

Waste away the day
In a furnished field of final straws
A corridor of open doors
Slamming shut.
Maybe that's the way?
If good things come to those who wait
We're feasting from a golden plate of
Ifs, maybes and buts.

Desire Line

Don't tell me where to go
With concrete made for walking
Don't tell me where to go
These boots will do the talking
There's a trail of trodden grass
That history will pass
From badgers' feet to mine
To mark the desire line
There's a trail of stone and soil
Compacted through a field
A natural-made short cut
A few more seconds to steal
And the seconds all add up
To minutes, hours and days
That we can spend together
Til we go our separate ways
There's a trail of broken hearts
That history will pass
One of them as mine:
The end of the desire line
Until death do us part
I'll walk that desire line
And when death do us part
There's still the desire line

Someone Scratched the Sky

Someone
Scratched the sky
They can't be in their right minds
They're going to cut our lifeline
Through to bone
Shall we climb up the hill
Then lie on our backs
And gaze into the stars on the wrong side of the tracks?
Someone
Scratched the sky
Are they trying to find a way out?
There's a better way to shout
You're not alone
If there'd been another day
If the weather hadn't changed
Would it still have been too late?
Could the two of us be saved?
Someone
Scratched the sky
Is that something in your eye?
Or have you changed your mind and it's not the end?

Street Art by Corvid

So,
When you said that life is too short
That inner beauty can't be bought
You knew I'd be an afterthought
And,
When I turned up, right on cue,
To say the things you needed me to,
To turn off the wringer that you'd been through
All that time, it turns out you knew
Then,
In the bitter aftermath
You said you'd thought it might be a laugh
And then you saw the get-out clause
Of towerblocks, and revolving doors
But,
When you said you'd made a film of our lives
I didn't think that I would be in disguise
Now I can't even look myself in the eye
I can't even look myself in the eye

Roasting on the Cobwebs

When it happens will it be like this?
There's no air passing.
When it happens will it be like this?
Breakwater, one man walks through the mist.
There's no air passing,
No lips moving.
Just close your eyes.
When it happens will I find peace?
Leave the harbour,
Sail to the east
Where in the morning
The sun will rise.
Just close your eyes.

Another Island

I can see your house
As the boat sets sail
And we leave the shore
As we both set sail
And we leave the shore
An approaching storm ...
There's a man
Overboard
If I had an idea
If I'd had the notion
I would find an island
In another ocean
If I had an island
In another ocean
Over by the rockpools
I would build a lighthouse

All is Well

Half past seven
Half past seven
All is well with the world
Half past seven
Made a decision
Turned off the television
All is well with the world
All is well with the world
All the flags are unfurled
It's just me and the birds
In this neck of the woods
Half past seven
Half past seven
All is well with the world

No Lego

No Lego, Meccano
No sticklebricks and bones
Your martyr, mere mortal
Built up with sticks and stones
And no-one ever sees it coming
A coast, a shore, a riverbed
No sticklebacks, no trout
No matter, you are mortal
We've come to fish you out
And no-one even sees it coming
These are the days
That fill your eyes
That catch you out
Your tongue in ties
These are the days
That fill your heart with stomach pits
These are the days
That fill your heart with
Lego bricks

No Ties

I'm thinking along a single track
I lost my way
So double back
If second thoughts are what I've got
I've got another think coming
She came over
Like a Royal visit I didn't see
I blinked
I missed it
With one more chance than I deserved
I lost my nerve
My head is where the war was fought
You know now
My nerves were taught
But I've got everything
Except what I'm missing
Too cocksure for sure
I learned my lesson well
I've got a way with words
But it's the wrong way

My Rusting Halo

Times I should have known better
Are racing round in my head
Like short, sharp shocks made of static,
Like junkshop dreams in the shed
Deepdive, into the river
Where pigeons are fished from the bed
Hopes pile high, in the attic,
Wrapped in layers of dread
Pay no heed
To my rusting halo
Shepherds fall from the ledge
Pay no heed
To my rusting halo
Don't stand close to the edge

As I Prepare Myself for the Battle Ahead

Fifteen feet from the garden fence
Standing firm with their armaments
There's a chip on my shoulder and a thorn in my side
The barbs are hidden in the bramble tide
I've dug my trench and I've earned my keep
It's an early grave and its ten feet deep
But I'm not going to give up easily
When there's cotton wool and there's TCP
I keep this thought at the back of my mind:
Scratch the surface, you don't know what you'll find
The wound is deep and my blood is red
But I'm not going to lose my head
It takes much more than a nick with a blade
It takes much more than a fork and a spade

Fake ID

There's something in the water
There's something in my eye
There's someone in the mirror
I used to recognise
There's something in the water
Or maybe in my genes
A little medication
Sometimes that's what you need
There's someone in the mirror
I used to recognise
I wonder what he's thinking
He looks a bit like me
Do you think that maybe it's a case of fake ID?

Sometimes You Don't Know Until it's Too Late

Somewhere in the pit of my mind
I dropped the key to how to live life
I'm trying hard to get it back
Detection is a skill that I lack
I'm not immune to knowing that it hurts
To see me when I know I'm at my worst
When silly things can cause me to fall
It's written all over your face
I don't enjoy behaving this way
I can't control the thoughts in my head
That make me feel... it's better not said
I don't blame you for looking so surprised
But some days I enjoy being alive
I love the warmth of sun on my skin
The effortless way the birds sing

Barry, Mick, Dot

Scrape your face from off the floor
Fingers bloated,
Knuckles sore
One more pint,
Or maybe four
And I wish you'd take some notice
Will you miss me when I'm dead
Do you think you'd even notice
You think that you might be our saviour
I'll cross your palm for years to come
I've seen you now
I'll raise you
Barry, Mick and Dot
Tie your fingers burn the knot
You're the lovers time forgot
And I think I owe you lots I owe you lots

Trevor Raines is Dead

I found the light
I was touched
Bythe hand of a child
On a pushbike
My collar was felt
In a lay-by,
Lured by a constable's
Sweet smile
I'm going away for a long time
There's a voice in my head saying "Goodbye"
I've spoken to god one or two times
"Trevor," he says, "you're a good guy"
But
My wife left me for her mother
My dog left me for my brother
With some luck
I might find a lover
With my luck
I don't think I'll bother

Find a Hill and Climb It

Is there more to life than breathing?
Is there more to life than breeding?
I cannot take in air
I've got my son and heir
Sometimes when I'm reminded
I get underexcited
Sometimes I'm undecided
Should I find a hill and climb it?
The third degree
Is guaranteed
The second that
I first fall
Silent

It's Not That Simple

If I could figure out
If I could understand
I wouldn't be sitting here with my head in my hands
I might be up
Living life to the hilt
Dancing round the house
In a Highland kilt
But
It's not that simple

One Day I'll Keep Walking

Living: it's not easy
When you go to work
Half-fed
You get home
Half-dead
And your mind is somewhere else
Inbetween
And you can't find the words
To capture the hurt
That you feel
Yet talking comes cheap
If you've
Nothing to say
Shut your trap, walk away
The moon hangs low in the sky tonight
Full of the glow of
The moors alight
As you sit and you wait
For the
Click
Of the gate that one day
Won't come
Because one day
I'll keep walking

Seagulls Over Sorrento

Sometimes I dread the summer
Sometimes
And sometimes the sea brings us closer
Sometimes
If I close my eyes
Sometimes it's me that is flying
Sometimes
On thermals, ducking and diving
Sometimes
If I close my eyes
There's seagulls over Sorrento
Sunshine over the bay
Seagulls
Over Sorrento
Sunshine
Dancing on waves
Seagulls over Sorrento
Take me to the sea

I Once Had a Dream but I'm All Right Now

Something doesn't seem right
But i can't make out
What's moving
In the shadows
By the lighthouse
And since I've been feeling
It's worse than it is
The fog's turned to drizzle
The cloud into mist
But nothing lasts forever
The snow on the ground
Will soon become river

Jack and Jilted

Bored of adores
Lets board up the doors
Turn down the lights
Get blind drunk
Majoring in
Plagiarism
Your baseball bat charm
Was my persuasion
With time to waste
With looks to kill
You walk on water
And pour our cares downhill
But when the heat is on
I find you're always long gone
And when I find my excuse
It's the wrong one
Sometimes you leave me wondering
What's left from what I put in
I had my doubts
You had the nerve
But I found out

We've Got the Photographs to Prove It

We've got the photographs to prove it
I saw you dancing in the aisles
With your shirt sleeves ripped
From the elbows down
You're living in Surroundsound
You made a negative impression
I saw you leaving by the back door
With a Persian rug
Wrapped around your shoulders
Like someone from Film on Four
But don't turn it back on me because you've been found out
Don't turn it back on me
You've been found out

Heading for the Sun

I smashed the bedroom window, and
Throughout the coming days
We lived in
Icy silence
Whilst waiting to be glazed.
When the glass was mended
Our hearts began to thaw.
Our new-found love confused me
So I started on the door.
I smashed the door to splinters;
You stuck them in my spine.
I rearranged your features;
You distorted mine.
When the war was ended a new day had begun.
We pushed our beds together and
Headed for the sun.
I smashed the bedroom window.
I smashed it with a chair.
I threw out your belongings
I cut off all my hair
When the war was ended I knew what I had done
I wrapped my arms around myself
I headed for the sun.

Something Borrowed

There's addresses
And names
And envelopes scattered
Once a boy loved a girl
In the same old way
Sometimes I think I might take a disguise
Put a face to a name
Put paper to flame
And watch it burn
There's a candle
By a window
Looking out
On the harbour
Once a girl loved a boy
Until her heart set sail
Washed up on the shore my plans hit a flaw
So I screamed at your door
"I can't take anymore
Please take me in
Again"
Something borrowed my heart
Something borrowed my hope
Pulled them two miles apart
And bound them with rope
And with a tortuous feather
Tickled them pink
Then drew them together
With invisible ink
As we looked for something borrowed
I thought of something new

We could go dressed
As each other
What's it like to be like you?

Quicksand

You make my skin crawl
There's no substitute for vitriol
Hammer me through your skin and bones
Fill my mouth with toxic foam
I know your weakness
I can't promise not to let
Your secrets
Slip out
Of my blabbermouth
Or be carved
As my epitaph
I'm sinking
From where I stand
I love your walls of quicksand
But take me to dry land
I can't comprehend
Where its going to end
I feel ill at ease
Give me your remedies
You've left me all at sea
And now I'm sinking

Pick Me Up

When you go
You stab me in the back
And I'm left
Stood in awe
At your put-me-downs
And all the time
You ask me what I'm thinking
Your ship's coming in
While I'm sat watching my ship
Sinking
Don't waste my time
It's the only thing worth keeping
I'll keep some for you
Because I know
That you
Will be needing some
Soon

Soberstars

You'll find me
In an empty bar
Staring into space
Not super
Not sober
Put firmly
In my place
I'm ozone-friendly
Affection-free
At half-past drinking-up time
I'm uptown
Downbeat
And fortified with beer
And cheap red wine
Meet me
Where the sky hits sea
Let trawlers
And pub-crawlers
Rescue me
Come pound-of-flesh collection time

Luggage in the Nose Cone

Suitcase
Rucksack
Golf clubs
Go-kart
Tent
Pushchair
Surfboard
Don't care:
Just put the luggage in the nose cone
Put the luggage in the nose cone

Arrivals and Departures

It's just
A little hut
But to me
It means
A lot

ATFC

Air
Traffic
Control
Freaks

Grass Runway

When the wind
Blows across
And lifts up
The fog
But the tarmac
Can't be reached
Don't land
Upon the beach
Use the
Grass runway

Waiting

I'm going nowhere
I'm staying put
We're going home
They're coming back
We're going home
Stop looking backwards
Stay awake
You said
It wouldn't matter
You said
It's okay
You daft old bastard

There Goes the Seaside

Buckets and spades
Seaweed and snails
Deck chairs and windbreaks
Ice creams and milkshakes
Bikes, trams and land trains
Windmills with white sails
Jellyfish at low tide
Sand dunes on both sides
Donkeys and postcards
Landlady's tabards
Sunburn and ozone
I don't want to go home

All is Not as it Seems

Give me a day
Give you a week
Give you a month
I'll take a year
I need to sleep
You need to breathe
I think we both need to disappear
To where the 'mares turn to dreams
And all is not as it seems
I need you
You need me
We made our own slice of history
Just look at you
Just look at me
We both need friends
Not an enemy
With half an mind on the sequel
Four-tracks on the floor
With half an eye on the split-screen
A tear drops in your ice cream
Switched on like a lightbulb
That's switched off at the wall
Which one is the right John
To stand up and perform
I miss you
Come back
Please
Don't come back
I need you
You don't need me

Give me an inch I'll take infinity
Just look at you
Just look at me
This isn't milk bottle sympathy

Chasing Last Year's Snow

And in the morning parliament
The beating of the wing
Came forth to signify that
We'd lost everything
What's done is done
And in the evening symphony
With horseshoe and a claw
Came darkness out of light
Nightfall out of dawn
Boxed in
Nowhere left to go
Don't go chasing last year's snow
And in the morning conference
Surrounded by a flood
Come forth the resolution
Just burn down the wood
And in the evening cabinet
Regret was not a choice
The best thing is silence
If you need to drown the voice

Try Not to Breathe

There's nothing you can say to me
That won't be voided in a week;
That creaking stair,
That creaking gate,
Under the sheets I'm fast awake
You didn't leave a trace behind;
At least, nothing that
Springs to mind,
But even so
I cannot sleep
My pulse is twenty to the beat
I'll try not to breathe
I'll try not to breathe
We feared the farmer's wrath
As we walked the farmer's path
And we feared the farmer's gun
As we crossed the field beyond
That contained the farmer's pond
Where we last fed the farmer's swan

Tinsel and Fabric

Lips dry
And i-Spy
I don't remember ...
I maybe said something
That was out of place
Once in a while
I would smile
Remember?
Much later on
I'm still none
The wiser
I'm trying to find a better state of mind
Trying to evade proposals she made
It's trying in vain
I should know
Peaceful seagulls
Become my witness
Hindsight is all right
But it makes me cry

Gullible's Travels

With your good looks
And my unlucky charms
We could make our living
Selling hand-me-downs
If you're killing time
I've plenty on my hands
Desperate times
Call for double measures
I can't accept these exotic treasures
I've had a bellyful of being me
I once had a heart
It turned to stone
I gave it to a man calling
'Rag and bone'

I Said 'No.'

Laughter today
At the night before
I'd spent all my time
Clutching at last straws
A drunken and desperate
Joke of a man
Top of the list of
The also-rans
My mind said 'Go!'
My body said 'No.'
I'm paying the price
It's begun to take its toll.
You said
'This boy will never learn.'
I said
'I'd rather wait than miss my turn.'
You said
'You're going to get your fingers burned.'
I said 'No.'

The World Outside

Sellotape my ears;
I can hear you leave
Putty in my ears?
I can feel you breathe
Superglue my hands;
I can smell your fear
Put a rubber in my nose but I won't disappear
I count degrees and minutes
I count for hours on end
Horizons are infinite
If you just avoid the bends
I count degrees and minutes
The hours and days respond
There's a world outside my window
I just can't see beyond

How Green Are Your Eyes?

For each
decision that you
take
There's a thousand
hearts you'll
break
For every
heart that you
break
There's a thousand
more at
stake
For every
heart that's at
stake
There's a million
you can't
shake
How green are your eyes in the sunrise?
How green are your eyes in the light?
How deep your regret in the sunset?
How deep your regret in the night?

Don't miss out!

Visit the website below and you can sign up to receive emails whenever John Hartley publishes a new book. There's no charge and no obligation.

https://books2read.com/r/B-A-HAEW-HHVIC

BOOKS 2 READ

Connecting independent readers to independent writers.

Did you love *Out of Tune*? Then you should read *Seasonal Adjustments*[1] by John Hartley!

[2]

Seasonal Adjustments is the first collection of poems written by John Hartley. Taking the reader through the year with a mix of humour and reflection, the anthology considers themes including the natural world, well-being, family and weather.

Although this is his first formal foray into the world of published poetry John's history is littered with rhyme, largely through lyrical writing to accompany musical melody. He grew up reading the works of McGough, Larkin, Rosen, Hughes, Hardy and Armitage. He won a certificate in an Observer young poetry competition at the age of 14 and once sang "I have a way with words but it's the wrong way". Find out here how true that is...

---

1. https://books2read.com/u/49LEaw

2. https://books2read.com/u/49LEaw

Also by John Hartley

Capturing The Wry
Seasonal Adjustments
Out of Tune

About the Author

John has written, performed and reviewed alternative music since the late 1980s. Founder member of cult band The Irony Board, he has continued to release music with Echolalia, Broken Down Lorry, The Broken Heed and most recently as Johny Nocash. He began reviewing music for the Neo-Tokyo online magazine in the mid 1990s, and has since written comprehensively for the acclaimed Dukla Prague Away Kit blog, the Everything Indie Over 40 website and Toppermost.

His memoir 'Capturing the Wry' was first published by i40Publishing in 2018. His forthcoming authorised biography of the indie band BOB is published by i40Publishing in February 2023.

When not filling his head with music John is a father of three, long-suffering supporter of Bolton Wanderers and Chorley FC, an enthusiastic drinker of tea, and a school leader in special education. He also writes Young Adult fiction.